What, Where, When, How, Why, and Who To Remember To Be Happy

What, Where, When, How, Why, and <u>Who</u> To Remember To Be Happy is formally authorized for publication by the Ruchira Sannyasin Order of the Tantric Renunciates of Adidam. (The Ruchira Sannyasin Order of the Tantric Renunciates of Adidam is the senior Spiritual and Cultural Authority within the formal gathering of formally acknowledged devotees of the Divine World-Teacher, Ruchira Avatar Adi Da Samraj.)

What, Where, When, How, Why, and <u>Who</u> To Remember To Be Happy is Part Two of Avatar Adi Da Samraj's Book of Spiritual Instruction for children and young people, *What, Where, When, How, Why, and <u>Who</u> To Remember To Be Happy: The Seventeen Companions Of The True Dawn Horse, Book Thirteen—A Simple Explanation Of The Divine Way Of Adidam (For Children, and <u>Everyone</u> Else)* (forthcoming from the Dawn Horse Press).

NOTE TO BIBLIOGRAPHERS:
The correct form for citing Ruchira Avatar Adi Da Samraj's Name (in any form of alphabetized listing) is:
Adi Da Samraj, Ruchira Avatar

Previously published as *What To Remember To Be Happy*
First Edition, February 1978
Children's Hardcover Edition, updated, February 2000

Produced by the Vision of Mulund Institute in cooperation with the Dawn Horse Press,
a division of the Eleutherian Pan-Communion of Adidam

Library of Congress Cataloging-in-Publication Data

Da Free John, 1939-
  What, where, when, how, why, and who to remember to be happy / by the
Divine World-Teacher, Ruchira Avatar Adi Da Samraj ; illustrations by
Maja van der Veer.
    p. cm.
  Rev. ed. of: What to remember to be happy. 1978.
  Summary: Leads readers through the contemplation of who we are, what we
know, what death is, and what true happiness is, focusing on the three
fundamental things to remember every day in order to be happy.
  ISBN 1-57097-074-2
  1. Spiritual life—Juvenile literature. [1. Spirituality.] I. Veer,
Maja van der, ill. II. Da Free John, 1939- What to remember to be happy.
III. Title.
  BP610.B8184 2000
  299'.93—dc21
                                00-008488

Book and Cover Design: Crowfoot Design
Printed in China by Palace Press International

What, Where, When, How, Why, and <u>Who</u> To Remember To Be Happy

By
The Divine World-Teacher,
RUCHIRA AVATAR ADI DA SAMRAJ

ILLUSTRATIONS BY MAJA VAN DER VEER

THE DAWN HORSE PRESS
MIDDLETOWN, CALIFORNIA

**H**ave you heard this is an apple?

Have you been told this is a tree?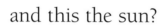

Do you think this is the moon?

and this the sun?

Have you told someone this is a little girl?

and this is a little boy?

Well. But you and I can be very truthful to each other.

And it seems to Me that, no matter what we name

this   or this

or this   or this

or this   or this

we still do not know what they <u>Are</u>. Truly, you and I don't know what even a single thing <u>Is</u>. Do you know what I <u>Am</u>? See? And I don't know what you <u>Are</u>, either. It is a Mystery. Doesn't it make you feel good to feel It?

D

id you ever ask somebody where

this   or this   or this   came from,

or how this   or this   or this   came to be?

Some say, "I don't know," and saying this makes them feel they are being
very honest and truthful. Others say something such as "God made it,"
or "It comes from God." And such people are also being very honest and
truthful when they say this.

How can they both be telling the truth? Well, because they are both telling you the same thing in different ways. You see, <u>nobody</u>—not Mom, or Dad, or Grandmother, or Grandfather, or big Sister, or big Brother, or teachers, or doctors, or soldiers, or athletes, or lawyers, or TV stars, or any people who are working, or any people who are playing, not even a President, not even a King or a Queen, not even people who love each other—<u>nobody</u> knows what even a single thing <u>Is</u>. It is a great and more-than-wonderful Mystery to everyone that anything <u>is</u>, or that we <u>are</u>. And whether somebody says "I don't know how anything came to be" or "God made everything", they are simply pointing to the feeling of the Mystery—of how everything <u>is</u>, but nobody knows what it really <u>Is</u>, or how it came to be.

11

As long as you go on feeling this Mystery, you feel free and full and

happy—and you feel and act free and full and happy to others. This is the

secret of being happy from the time you are small until the time you are old.

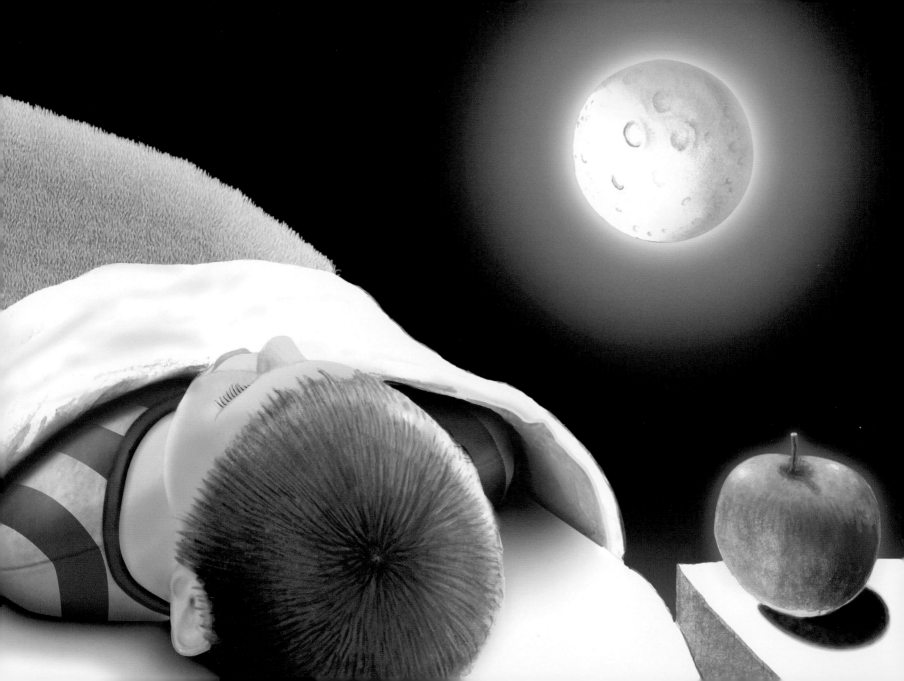

Everybody—even all the animals—goes on living for a while, and then the part of them you see and touch and talk to every day when you wake up goes to sleep in the feeling of the Mystery. This happens to everybody. And everybody has to live every day without being afraid to go to sleep. This can be difficult, even when you are small. Especially because people sometimes forget the Mystery, and get unhappy, and try to make others feel unhappy—by making them think things that make them afraid and make them forget the Mystery.

So the way to keep on being happy every day until you go to sleep is to

remember the Mystery. Just keep on remembering that you, with everybody

else, do not know what even a single thing <u>Is</u>—not even an

Just remember this—or remember Real God, which is the same thing.
Keep on remembering Real God as the Mystery, and you will feel happy and
act happy to others—and so you will keep on loving and helping others, so
the world won't get all afraid, and stupid, and unable to sleep or play or work.

If you do this all the time, you will have lots of amazing and more-than-wonderful experiences until you go back to sleep. And, if you remember the Mystery even when you are going to sleep, then you will go to sleep all happy in the Mystery. And you will always wake up in the Mystery, too. And all your dreams will be about the Mystery, until you wake up again.

Remembering the Mystery is a way of being everything you always already <u>are</u>. When you sleep, you are something different than when you wake up. And when you dream, you are different, too. The way you seem to be when you wake up is only <u>one</u> of the ways you are.

Some day, everybody has what they look like go to sleep and not wake up. Then they forget that part, and they go on to someplace else and look different. Nobody knows what they will look like after what they look like now goes to sleep forever. When you go to sleep at night, you forget what you looked like all day. And when somebody dies, or lets the body go to sleep for the last time, they forget what they looked like when they were alive and awake. It is a Mystery— like going to sleep, or dreaming, or waking up.

So, whether you look like or you are not only the way you look.

Well. If you are going to stay happy and keep on loving and not be afraid, there are <u>three</u> good things to remember lots of times all day every day, and at special sitting-and-doing-nothing-else-but-this times every day.

These three good things to remember are <u>three</u> ways of remembering the Mystery— or staying the way you really <u>Are</u> before you start to name things and think and know about anything.

Before you name or think or know, you already <u>Are</u> and you already <u>feel</u>.

The first thing to remember a lot when you are awake (or even dreaming, or who knows what) is to <u>feel</u> the Mystery, and so <u>feel</u> Reality—or the One and Only Real God. Feel that you don't <u>know</u> what even a single thing <u>Is</u>. You may know the name of something or someone. You may know about all kinds of somethings and someones. But you do not—and you cannot—<u>know</u> what anything or anyone <u>Is</u>. Nobody does— and nobody can. It is important to remember and feel this a lot. When you do this, you feel quiet, and you forget all the names, and you forget to be afraid, and you stop thinking—and you only feel good, and true, and full of love, and radiating.

And when you feel the Mystery real strong, you can tell that you even breathe the Mystery. When people feel the Mystery real strong and breathe It, they say things like "God is Spirit"—because "Spirit" is just a name for what people feel about their breath. When people say things like this, they are only feeling very happy. They don't know anything more than before about Real God. They are just wondering beyond wondering—how the Mystery even goes all through them, and doesn't have any shape or face or up or down or inside or outside.

Well. When you remember to feel the Mystery real strong, then you can also remember to breathe the Mystery. The Mystery is good feeling, full of light and happiness and love—isn't It? So, when you breathe the Mystery, remember always to breathe in all the good feeling and breathe out all the bad feeling.

Breathe in all the happy feeling about the Mystery, and breathe out all the unhappy feelings you might be thinking about—like being afraid, or angry, or selfish, or mean, or just unhappy. Stand up, and feel to yourself: "Breathe in the good stuff—Breathe out the bad stuff." And do this feeling-breathing, in and out, again and again. It is good to do this, every now and then—every day. It is a way to get to remember the Mystery stronger and stronger. And, if you remember the Mystery stronger and stronger, you start to feel so good after a while that it seems like you aren't remembering and feeling and breathing the Mystery anymore—but the Mystery is remembering and feeling and breathing <u>you</u>!

What A Mysterious Great Happy Mystery The Mystery <u>Is</u>!

27

The second thing to remember a lot every day is that you are always more than what you <u>look</u> like. The part that is the way you look is only you while you are awake and alive. But the rest of you goes on while you sleep and dream—and, after the body dies (or goes to sleep for good), the rest of you goes on in the Mystery. The way to remember this is to see and feel <u>everything</u> that is yourself, all the time. The <u>body</u> part of you—the way you look when you are awake—is only <u>part</u> of the way you are. You also <u>feel</u> and <u>think</u> when you are awake, and when you dream (even though the body is forgotten in dreams). But even more than this is the way you can feel yourself to be in the Mystery.

It is a good idea, along with remembering to feel the Mystery all the time, to sit down quiet and not busy every day for a little or a big while. Feel the Mystery real strong, and breathe It—until your breathing becomes real quiet, and you are <u>only</u> feeling the Mystery—really quiet and strong. Then close your eyes, and put one of your fingers in each ear—so you can't hear any noises in the room or outside your face. Then listen inside. Listen up toward the top of your head, with your eyes closed. Try it now—and then come back to reading again.

Well. Did you hear? All the sounds inside your face? There is ringing and tinkling, and popping and tapping and fluting, and thumping like a xylophone, and strumming and drumming, and ocean roaring, and waterfalling, and booming and buzzing, and all kinds of sounds like birds and crickets and bees and music, and a big deep humming all over, and some kind of feeling way up that you cannot even hear, and especially lots of quiet, too.

N ow put a finger over each eye, with your eyes closed and looking up inside toward the top of your head. Try it now—and then come back to reading again.

Did you see? There are lights, and zigzags, and lightning, and stars, and moving shiny spots, and shivering shapes, and all kinds of spaces and moons and suns (and even places), and all kinds of things to see—like in dreams, and really, too.

It is good and fun and Mysterious to do this with your ears and eyes every day—so you will remember to feel what you are that is more than what you look like. You are electrical, and you are light and sound—whatever all of that may be. If people don't forget to feel this, they stay happy, and not afraid to love or to die—and they go on and on.

So far, you have two things to remember a lot every day.

First: Remember to feel the Mystery, and even breathe It. Second: Remember to feel you are more than what you look like. (And a good way to do this is to sit and relax and feel the Mystery with your ears and eyes closed up at the same time—like when you are asleep.)

The third thing it is good to remember every day is that you do the feeling and breathing and listening and looking and naming all the time. You aren't anything you know or feel or see or hear or look like or name or think. All these things just happen—and you get to watch or know or think them. You feel and see your own body. You feel and see your inside sounds or lights or dreams—or all the places that come up.

You think the names of [apple] and [tree] and [moon] and [sun] and [child] and [child].

You even think "I", and "me", and "mine". Well, what <u>are</u> you, if you only <u>watch</u> all of these things?

You <u>Are</u> the Mystery! <u>Yes</u>! And you don't even know what <u>you</u> <u>Are</u>, either. <u>Yes</u>! There <u>Is</u> <u>Only</u> the Mystery! And you yourself—in your Real Heart, and up and down and in and out—<u>Are</u> the Mystery. It <u>Is</u> All <u>One</u> <u>Feeling</u>!

If you will remember every day to feel and breathe the Mystery, and if you will remember to feel that you are more than what you look like, and if you will remember to <u>Be</u> the Mystery Itself—then you will be happy every day. And all kinds of more-than-wonderful happenings will come up for you. You will feel happy, and you will always help and love others—even those who are having trouble feeling happy, and are even trying to make you forget the Mystery.

It is good to spend a lot of your time talking about the Mystery with others—instead of talking about unhappiness and things that happen when you forget to love. People who also feel the Mystery and love It are the best friends to have—because they always remind you to feel the Mystery, and to be happy, and to love.

I have always been remembering and feeling and breathing and loving and <u>Being</u> the Mystery. And I was born so that I could be <u>everyone's</u> Friend— by Showing them the Mystery, and Teaching them about the Mystery, and Helping them to remember and feel and breathe and love and <u>Be</u> the Mystery.

Happiness is the now-and-forever Mystery that <u>Is</u> the Real Heart and the Only Real God of every one.

I am the "Bright" Teacher of Happiness—the Ruchira Avatar, Adi Da Samraj, the Divine Heart-Master of all and All.

I have Come from the Heart of every one.

I Am in (and in front of) the Heart of every one.

Because I <u>Am</u> the Real Heart <u>Itself</u>, I will <u>always</u> forever be remembering and feeling and breathing and loving and <u>Being</u> the Mystery—for <u>you</u>.

E ven <u>all</u> My friends can easily always forever remember and feel and breathe and love and <u>Be</u> the Mystery—if only they remember <u>Me</u>, and feel <u>Me</u>, and breathe <u>Me</u>, and love <u>Me</u>.

Therefore, all My friends should <u>constantly</u> forget themselves, and forget their unhappiness, and forget even what they look like—and remember <u>only</u> <u>Me</u>.

Now, and forever hereafter, those who truly and completely remember <u>only</u> <u>Me</u> will find it easy to remember to <u>Be</u> the Mystery—because I <u>Am</u> the Mystery Itself.

And I Am even Shown <u>As</u> a Man here—so that it will always be easy for you to remember Me—Always Already "Bright" and here, for one and all and All—forever.

Vegetable Surrender or Happiness Is Not Blue

This humorous and instructive story was written by Adi Da Samraj for young children. In it, Onion One-Yin and his vegetable friends embark on a search for someone who can help them solve their problems— and discover the secret of how to be happy, right now!

Illustrated with line drawings. 10-3/4" x 8-3/4" hardcover, 46 pages. Black and white illustrations. **$10.00**

To order this book, or to request a free catalog with other literature by and about Adi Da Samraj and Adidam, contact:

1-877-770-0772
(within North America)

(707) 928-6653
(outside North America)

Order on-line: www.adidam.com

The Adidam Emporium
10336 Loch Lomond Road #306
Middletown, CA 95461 USA

For More Information About Avatar Adi Da Samraj

Visit the Adidam website: www.adidam.org
- See photographs of Avatar Adi Da
- Hear audio-clips of Him speaking
- Read His writings and stories of His Divine Work
- Find a complete listing of Adidam regional centers worldwide

Read *The Promised God-Man Is Here*, the full story of the life and work of Avatar Adi Da Samraj, written for adults.

Order from the Adidam Emporium:

877-770-0772
within North America

707-928-6653
outside North America

www.adidam.com

For more information about Avatar Adi Da's Wisdom relative to conscious childrearing please write or call:

The Vision of Mulund Institute
10336 Loch Lomond Road #146
Middletown, CA 95461 USA
(707) 928-6932

E-MAIL: vmi@adidam.org

Contact an Adidam regional center:

Americas
12040 North Seigler Road
Middletown, CA 95461 USA
(707) 928-4936

Pacific-Asia
12 Seibel Road
Henderson, Auckland 1008
New Zealand
64-9-838-9114

Europe-Africa
Annendaalderweg 10
6105 AT Maria Hoop
The Netherlands
31-(0)20-468-1442

Australia
P.O. Box 460
Roseville, NSW 2069
Australia
61-2-9419-7563

United Kingdom
P.O. Box 20013
London, England NW2 1ZA
0181-731-7550

E-MAIL: correspondence@adidam.org